Tracing Our
POLISH
Roots

SHARON MOSCINSKI

John Muir Publications
Santa Fe, New Mexico

John Muir Publications, P.O. Box 613, Santa Fe, NM 87504

Printed in the United States of America

First edition. First printing July 1994
        First TWG printing July 1994

Library of Congress Cataloging-in-Publication Data
Moscinski, Sharon.
American origins: tracing our Polish roots / by Sharon Moscinski.
   p.   cm.
   Includes index.
   ISBN 1-56261-161-5 : $12.95
1. Polish Americans—History—Juvenile literature. [1. Polish Americans—History. 2. United States—Emigration and immigration.] I. Title.
E184.P7M72 1994
973'.049185—dc20   93-50732
                                                         CIP
                                                         AC

Logo design: Peter Aschwanden
Illustrations: Anthony D'Agostino
Typography: Jim Wood
Printer: Arcata Graphics / Kingsport

Distributed to the book trade by
W. W. Norton & Co., Inc.
500 Fifth Avenue
New York, New York 10110

Distributed to the education market by
The Wright Group
19201 120th Avenue N.E.
Bothell, WA 98011-9512

Cover photo, Joseph Boleslaw Slotkowski, founder of the Slotkowski Sausage Company,
  Chicago, 1918 © The Kosciuszko Foundation
Title page photo, a young Polish American worker at the Quidnick Mills, Rhode Island, 1911
  © The Kosciuszko Foundation
Back cover photo, Polish American wedding photo, Niagara Falls, 1919 © The Kosciuszko
  Foundation

CONTENTS

THE ADVENTURE BEGINS

Poles have been coming to America for centuries—since the early 1600s, in fact. The first Polish immigrants were highly trained craftsmen. They were invited to America by the English settlers to lend their skills to the growing colonies. These Poles dug ditches, cleared the land, and built small factories to make such products as soap, tar, and glass. Their work helped many colonies, especially Jamestown and New Amsterdam (now New York City), grow and thrive.

Next, a small but steady flow of Polish immigrants came to America between 1780 and 1860. During this time Poland was not a free country but was controlled by three neighboring countries, Austria, Russia, and Prussia (Germany). Many of the Polish patriots who fought to free Poland became political exiles, meaning they had to flee Poland to escape imprisonment or death.

Most of the Polish exiles settled in nearby European countries, but some braved the wide Atlantic and made America their new home. Many of these Polish immigrants fought heroically for the

How Many Poles Came to America?

Decade	Number
1861–1870	2,027
1871–1880	12,970
1881–1890	51,806
1891–1900	96,720
1901–1910	*1 million
1911–1920	*1 million
1921–1930	227,734
1931–1940	17,026
1941–1950	157,571
1951–1960	9,985
1961–1970	53,539
1971–1980	37,234

*From 1899 to 1919, records of Polish immigrants were not kept. Instead, Poles were listed as immigrants from Austria-Hungary, Germany, and Russia. However, it is estimated that more than 2 million Poles came to America during this period. Also, an estimated 150,000 Polish refugees immigrated to the United States after World War II.

The Bettmann Archive

Polish peasants in traditional costume

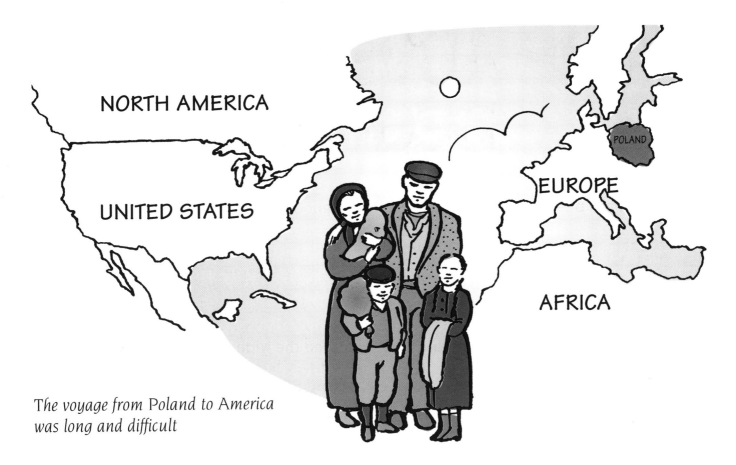

NORTH AMERICA

UNITED STATES

EUROPE

POLAND

AFRICA

The voyage from Poland to America was long and difficult

colonies against the British during the Revolutionary War. Others became respected writers, artists, and educators. Still others came to America for adventure and travel. They pioneered the West and befriended Indians, or they flocked to the California hills during the Gold Rush of 1849.

Our story focuses mainly on the Poles who immigrated to America between 1880 and 1925. During this period, about 3 million Poles poured onto America's shores. Most were poor farmers who sought to improve their lives. They had no money, few skills, and little education. But they had a dream that in America their hard work would earn them a better life. Usually it did, but it often took a lifetime to achieve.

Poles endured many hardships in America, but the New Country offered them something they did not have back in Poland—hope. Most immigrants worked long hours in sweatshops, day after day,

year after year. But every now and then they heard a success story, and this encouraged them to strive for their dreams.

Perhaps a Polish cousin had just opened a bakery and was making a little money, or a friend owned a successful farm in New England. Even Polish immigrants who worked in city factories for more than thirty years often saved enough money to buy their own home at last. America was not a paradise, but it was a land that granted poor people a chance for a better life.

Tracing Our Polish Roots tells the story of the Polish immigrants who gave up everything for the American dream. These immigrants left behind their families, churches, villages—everything except one trunkful of possessions. They spent two weeks seasick inside the cramped hulls of ships. And they landed in an unfamiliar country they had never even seen in pictures, where the people spoke a strange language it would take years to understand.

3

POLISH HISTORY

Poland was founded as a nation in A.D. 966, when the Polish ruler Mieszko (mee-ESH-koh) I brought Christianity to Poland.

After Mieszko I, one of the next imp ortant Polish kings was Casimir (KAHS-eh-meer) the Great. He ruled Poland from 1333 to 1370. Casimir took advantage of the peace during his reign to improve the economy and unify the laws of the country. In 1364, he founded the University of Krakow. It served as a great European center of learning for centuries.

Casimir's grandniece, Jadwiga (yahd-VEE-gah), married Jagiełło (yah-GEL-oh) of Lithuania in 1386. This marriage united Poland and Lithuania and began the powerful Jagiellonian (yah-GEL-own-ee-an) dynasty, which lasted more than 200 years.

The Jagiełło rulers were known for their religious tolerance. Under their reign, Catholics, Protestants, Jews, and Orthodox Christians lived peacefully together in Poland. However, during this time many other parts of Europe were fighting religious wars. But because Poland was peaceful, it was able to become a wealthy country as well as the European center for literature, science, and the arts.

In 1572, the Jagiellonian dynasty ended and the Polish Republic was created. The Polish parliament, called the Sejm (same),

---

Even though Poland had been wiped off the map as its own country, the Polish people clung to their language, their religion, and their land. They formed groups so their culture and history would be kept alive by future generations. As a result, the Poles preserved much of their heritage during 122 years of foreign rule.

The first partition of Poland, in 1772

The second partition of Poland, in 1793

The third partition of Poland, in 1795

The Polish winged cavalry charges into battle

now ruled the nation. The Sejm ran very well until it passed an act in 1652 that declared *all* members of Parliament had to agree on a law in order for it to be passed.

But how could so many people be expected to agree completely on every issue? It was an impossible task, and the Sejm became disorganized. As a result, the Polish army shrank in size, education reached its lowest level, and fights over religion became more common. Poland became a weak nation.

Poland's neighbors—Russia, Prussia, and Austria—knew Poland no longer had the military strength to resist an invasion. So the three nations worked together to divide and conquer Poland piece by piece.

The first two divisions occurred in 1772 and 1793. After the second division, all that was left of Poland was an area about the size of a large city. The outraged Polish people began a nationwide campaign to take back their country. In 1794, Thaddeus Kosciuszko (KOS-eh-US-koh) bravely led a national uprising. But with no allies, Poland could not defeat her three powerful neighbors.

Finally, in 1795, Poland was divided for the third and last time. Now all of the land that had once been Poland was claimed by either Russia, Prussia, or Austria. The Poles were forced to live under foreign rule. At various times, Poland was allowed to have some form of government, but it did not exist as an independent country again until after World War I (1914–1918).

POLISH PEASANTS

In the 1800s, more than one half of Poland was farmland, and more than three-fourths of the population were farmers. Most farm families lived in one of the thousands of small villages scattered throughout the country.

In a typical village, houses were built along both sides of a long road, and the fields were located in the back. The great dream of all Polish peasants was to own land, and then more land.

Families who owned their farms were respected in their community. They were even addressed by a special title, *gospodarz* (gos-PO-dazh) or *gospodyni* (gos-POHD-nyee). The landless peasants were called the *komorniki* (koh-mor-NEE-kee). They were tenant farmers, renting rather than owning their farms, and were considered just above beggars.

But owning land was difficult for the Polish peasant. Half of the farmable land in the entire country was owned by the nobility, who made up only one percent of the population. The farms left for the peasants to buy were often less fertile, and almost always too small to support a family.

The peasants struggled to make a living from their farms, and husband, wife, and children spent long hours toiling in the fields. Despite their hard work, the peasant farmers were usually in debt, meaning they owed money. To pay their bills, farmers had to sell their produce immediately, even if they could not get a fair price.

Peasant farmers could sometimes earn more money by working in the cities, but few made this choice. Status and family pride came not from wealth or how many things the family owned, but from how

Aging Polish parents often moved in with one of their children

It was Polish custom for the father to retire when his sons were able to manage the land themselves. The father might repeat the saying, "I have worked enough in my lifetime, now I may retire on my children," but it was an unhappy day when he had to part with his land. The parents usually moved into the home of their favorite child, and were cared for for the rest of their lives. But sometimes they were seen by their children as a burden and were mistreated. As a result, retiring parents often had their children sign a contract to honor them in their old age, at the risk of being cursed by God.

Some farm families owned livestock, especially cows, goats, and pigs

many acres they had—and the more, the better! Despite the hardships of farm life, the Poles clung to their land with love. They would sell their livestock, take out loans, or even go hungry before parting with their beloved land.

Next to the land, the heart of peasant Poland was the family. Families typically lived in a one-room hut. The outside was often whitewashed, the inside clean, and the roof thatched with straw. The homes of most Polish peasants were simple and had few pieces of furniture. They were the center of family life.

Yet Polish parents were not overly affectionate with their older children, and they did not coddle them. Parents expected every member of the family to work. Children cared for their younger siblings, tended to the livestock, helped with chores, and were respected most of all for their usefulness.

During the autumn harvest, entire families worked long hours in the fields

7

THE CHILDREN'S POLAND

Newborn babies in Poland were always the center of attention. They were pampered by their mothers, cuddled by relatives, and constantly rocked—otherwise, many peasants believed, the child would grow up to have shaky hands.

The christening of a newborn was one of the most festive events in the entire village. At one Polish christening, everyone became so merry (and most likely drunk!) that on the way home the parents realized their newly christened child had been forgotten back at the tavern!

Once Polish children began to toddle around, they were treated as miniature adults by their parents. Children became respected members of the household and were given different tasks at every age. It was not unusual for a five-year-old boy to rock the cradle, feed his younger siblings,

The Bettmann Archive

Polish children helped with family chores. Here, young Poles gather beets.

and do many household chores while his parents were toiling in the fields.

At age seven, girls and boys were considered old enough to tend the cattle. They woke at five in the morning and led the cattle to a lush pasture to graze. This was hard

In the evenings, village children often gathered together to talk about their days. These lively sessions always included sunflower seeds—a popular treat, like chewing gum is today. Instead of blowing bubbles, Polish children would show off the neat and complicated ways they could crack the seeds.

Sunflower seeds were a real treat to Polish kids

work for small children, and they could not play games to pass the time because they would be punished if a cow wandered off. But cattle tending was also exciting for children. They were given new, warm clothing, and were proud to handle such large animals all by themselves.

Polish parents tried to send their children to school, but it was often impossible for them to do so. Children were needed to work on the farm. And in the winter, when they had fewer farm chores, it was usually too cold to walk to the nearest school—often in a neighboring village.

As a result, most peasant children learned only the basics of reading and writing. But all Polish mothers wanted one of their sons to become a priest. So if a boy showed special intelligence, he alone would be sent to school full-time and encouraged to enter the priesthood.

But Polish children did not have to work all the time. In the evening, they romped through the fields, or played chase, charades, or a variation of tug-of-war called "The Devil and the Angel." If the side of the angel won, everyone would kiss and dance, but if the devil won, everyone would fall to the ground and pretend to fight.

Children also celebrated the many feast days, dances, and fairs that occurred throughout the year. The favorite events were the spinning and harvesting parties in the autumn and winter, which also featured storytelling.

The storytellers were often old beggars who picked up wild and wonderful tales on their many travels. They delighted and sometimes terrified their wide-eyed audiences with stories of heroes, devils, saints, and spirits. Afterwards, the children formed their own group and retold the stories—or just made up new ones—until the "cock crow called them back to work in the morning."

The Bettmann Archive

Some farmers used horses to help plow the fields before planting

POLISH CULTURE

Polish peasants, even the most successful ones, worked hard their entire lives. But the harshness of everyday life was softened by a rich folk culture. Song, dance, weaving, wood carving, paper cutting, egg coloring, and other arts and crafts were very important to Polish peasants, and were sources of ethnic pride.

Folk dancing was the most cherished national pastime. No festivity was complete if the participants did not dance till their feet ached. Many regional dances were known throughout Poland, but the lively *mazurka* (mah-ZUR-kah) was the most popular.

Everyone was encouraged to dance the *mazurka*, young and old alike, but the young men often stole the stage. These performers would spin, kick, crouch, and then leap to dazzling heights. Although people of many nationalities danced the *mazurka*, it was said none could fly through its measures like the native Pole.

Polish harvesters in their regional costume

Dances were great excuses to dress up. Each region in Poland had its own unique costume, but almost all were adorned with red and white—the national colors of Poland. Women and men both wore fancy headgear, and as a general rule, the more piled on the head, the better. The headdress of a young girl might sport flowers, feathers, beads, rib-

Pisanki, *decorated eggs, are a traditional Polish folk art*

According to a Polish legend, Mary Magdalene was carrying a basket of eggs when she went to visit Jesus' tomb. Later, when she told the apostles that Christ had risen, they did not believe her. She then showed them the eggs, which turned into beautifully decorated *pisanki* right before their eyes. The apostles finally believed Mary Magdalene when nightingales hatched from the *pisanki* singing "Alleluia!"

bons, tinsel, and other ornaments, and often reached spectacular heights.

Poland also had one of Europe's richest folk art traditions. Wood carvings were made by rural farmers, who spent the long winters carving figures with pocket knives. Most carvings featured saints, stories from the Bible, or scenes of everyday life. But wooden dolls, dressed in traditional peasant costumes, were also popular toys for children.

Egg decorating was perhaps the oldest Polish folk art. Decorated eggs were called *pisanki* (pi-SAHN-kee). Archaeologists have found eggshells that were decorated over a thousand years ago! To make *pisanki*, designs were drawn onto an eggshell in wax. The designs were of flowers, hearts, triangles, stars, household objects, or geometric patterns.

Next, the rest of the eggshell was dyed, usually in a deep, dark color. But the designs drawn in wax did not hold the dye, so they appeared as the original color of the eggshell against a colored background. A tiny hole was then pierced through the top and bottom of the egg, and the egg contents were carefully blown out of the shell.

Cutting paper for decoration, called *wycinanki* (vy-sin-AHN-kee), was another favorite Polish folk art. It started in the rural homes of Poland in the early 1800s, after paper became available throughout the country. Most families did not have scissors. They had to make their *wycinanki* using large, clumsy sheep shears. Even so, the skilled Poles were able to cut out beautiful, delicate, and complex designs.

Both *pisanki* and *wycinanki* decorated homes on Christmas, Easter, and other special occasions. The whole family helped create the decorations, and then they hung them from the ceilings or on the walls, windows, and cupboards throughout the house.

Playing music was a popular pastime in rural towns and villages

11

RELIGION

In the 1800s, 95 percent of the Polish population was Catholic. Poland was also home to a large Jewish community. Polish Catholics generally did not fight over religious ideas as people did in other European countries. To them, religion was simple, mysterious, and beautiful. Their strong faith kept their spirits alive in times of hardship.

After working hard for six days, the peasants rested on the seventh. Sundays were days of celebration. Families dressed in their very best and proudly paraded down to the local church.

The village churches were usually small, but inside they were mystical and awe-inspiring. Images of saints decorated the walls, statues gazed down upon the parishioners, and candles dimly lit the rooms. Within the church walls the peasants humbly knelt in prayer and found relief from the hardships of their daily lives.

The church also served as a community gathering center. The entire village participated in the Masses, feast days, and processions held throughout the year. After Mass the parishioners were cheery and refreshed. Sometimes they stayed at the church for hours to mingle and gossip.

When a member of the community died, the villagers formed a long line outside of the deceased's home and

Peasants sprinkled grain on their winter fields to guarantee a good harvest

Many Polish customs were part of religious holidays, especially the Christmas Eve dinner, called W*igilia* (vi-GEE-lee-ah). The dinner began when the first star in the sky was spotted. Hay was placed under the tablecloth to symbolize the manger where Christ was born, and the tablecloth was white like Mary's veil. Wafers called *oplatki* (ohp-LAHT-kee) were broken and shared. This was a time to patch up arguments and forgive people. Many peasants put the scales of the Christmas dinner fish in their purses "to keep the purse full of money in the coming year." And after dinner, they sprinkled wheat, rye, oats, and barley in their fields to guarantee a good harvest.

chanted, wept, beat their breasts, and prayed. In the springtime, the parish priest led his parishioners around the boundaries of the village. The procession chanted, rang bells, and recited prayers for a bountiful harvest.

The local parish was funded by the villagers themselves. Every so often, the priest went house to house asking for donations. Even during times of extreme poverty, the Poles freely gave contributions. But the Poles were especially generous when their harvest was good or on special holidays. Religion was the heart of the community, family, and individual in Poland, and the peasants believed few things deserved the profits of their labor more than their local parish.

To the Poles, the Virgin Mary symbolized kindness, understanding, and compassion. She in particular was worshiped throughout the country. The most sacred

Peasants from all over came to see the Black Madonna

Church of the Holy Cross, Warsaw

place in all of Poland was the Mother of God Church in Częstochowa (CHEN-sto-KOH-vah). Here hung the world-famous painting of the Virgin and Jesus called the *Black Madonna*. According to religious legend, it was painted by Saint Luke

shortly after Christ was resurrected into heaven.

Each year, peasants from all over Poland made a pilgrimage to see the *Black Madonna*. The pilgrimage often took more than a week, and the adventure was a welcome break from their heavy farm work. Once they arrived, the peasants asked the *Black Madonna* to cure an illness, help a loved one, or grant a special wish. Indeed, many miracles throughout Poland were said to have been performed by the power of the *Black Madonna*.

THE INTELLIGENTSIA

From 1795 until 1917—for 122 years—Poland did not exist as a country. Russia, Prussia, and Austria had divided Poland into three sections, and each country took one of these sections for itself. Once Poland was divided, many rights and privileges were taken away from the intelligentsia (in-tell-eh-JENT-see-ah), the wealthy landowners, nobility, and well-educated Poles.

The harshness of foreign rule varied in the different divisions of Poland. For example, in Prussian Poland it was illegal to speak Polish, and by law all schools had to be taught in German. As a result, noblewomen started secret home schools taught entirely in Polish. But if the Prussian police discovered these schools, the women were arrested, thrown in jail, and all of their Polish books would be burned.

Russian Poland was worse. Usually there were no schools at all. Also, police officers sat in on Catholic masses to make sure nothing was said against the Russian government. The intelligentsia was the most free in Austrian Poland, but even there Poles were downtrodden and angry.

In all parts of divided Poland, the Polish upper classes lost many privileges, including freedom of speech. Polish leaders were often jailed for being revolutionaries. In later years, universities were closed, and the wealthier Poles had to pledge allegiance to their conquerors.

Polish peasants often resented wealthy Poles

Generally, Polish peasants did not participate in revolutionary activities. And if they did, it was often *against* the intelligentsia! Why did the peasants fight against their own people? Because for centuries the Polish upper classes had oppressed the peasants. Before the 1800s, the peasants were serfs, meaning they had to work on their masters' land and had few, if any, rights as citizens. Russia, Prussia, and Austria, however, wanted to keep the Polish peasants happy. These countries knew that if the millions of peasants rebelled against them, they never could remain in control of Poland. As a result, many peasants had more freedom and a better life when ruled by foreigners than they did when ruled by Polish landowners!

This made them furious. While the peasants were especially loyal to their native village, the intelligentsia was loyal to Poland as a nation. As a result, the intelligentsia planned uprisings, rallies, and secret meetings. But when Poland was completely overthrown in 1795, thousands of Polish revolutionaries fled the country in what was called the "Great Emigration." They settled in many different countries—including America—and created a buzzing worldwide movement to "free Poland."

Abroad, Poles never lost faith that one day they would be able to return to a free and liberated Poland. Many exiles fought for the independence of other countries throughout the world. They were admired and respected as brave soldiers.

Many exiled poets, writers, and musicians spent their lives championing Polish freedom in their work. And Polish politicians never let Europe forget that Poland was unfairly suffering under foreign rule.

Upper-class Poles sometimes started secret home schools

These patriots were key players in keeping the Polish national spirit alive, until Poland was once again made an independent nation after World War I.

The city of Gdansk, occupied by Germany, became a part of Poland after World War I

THREE FAMOUS POLES

Nicolaus Copernicus (1473–1543)

Nicolaus Copernicus (koh-PUR-neh-kus) was born in eastern Poland in 1473. He studied mathematics, astronomy, medicine, and theology (the study of religion), but astronomy proved to be his true passion.

Copernicus learned the ancient astronomer Ptolemy's version of astronomy. Ptolemy (TAHL-uh-mee) believed that the Earth was the motionless center of the universe and that all of the other planets and heavenly bodies, including the sun, revolved around it.

Nicolaus Copernicus, a famous Polish astronomer

But after observing the motions of the planets himself, Copernicus concluded that Earth was not the center of the universe after all. He concluded that each day the Earth revolved around its own axis, and each year it revolved around the motionless sun.

Today Copernicus' theory may seem simple (and correct!), but in his day it caused quite a stir. Most people believed that humans were the center of Creation. And to prove it, they believed, Earth was placed smack in the center of the universe. But if Copernicus' claim were true, that meant that the Earth was just an ordinary planet—and humans weren't so special after all!

Copernicus' discovery upset a lot of people, and it forced many great thinkers to reexamine their beliefs. As a result, many advances were made in science and philosophy after the "Copernican Revolution."

Frederic Chopin (1810–1849)

Frederic Chopin (show-PAHN) was born in a village west of Warsaw in 1810. A musical genius, Chopin gave his first public piano performance at the age of eight. At 15, he played for the Tsar of Russia, and at 16, he began to study music at the Warsaw Conservatory. Chopin's delicate, refined, and romantic piano style won him fame and admiration throughout Europe.

Chopin left Poland in 1830 to settle with other artists in Paris. He never returned to his homeland. After an uprising in Poland

Frederic Chopin, Poland's greatest pianist and composer

against the Russian Tsar, the Poles were treated worse than ever. The quality of art, literature, and music in Poland declined, and the Warsaw Conservatory, where Chopin was schooled, was forced to close. There was no longer a place for Chopin's talent in Poland.

Even so, Chopin clung to his Polish roots. His compositions were often inspired by the folk rhythms, melodies, and national dances of his native land. He kept the soul of Poland alive and strong in his music. Chopin died in Paris in 1839, and his music has ever since been considered "the finest art Poland ever produced."

Marie Curie (1867–1934)

Marie Sklodowska-Curie (sklah-DOF-skah cure-EE) was born in Warsaw in 1867. She was an extraordinary child who could read by the age of four. Fascinated by the workroom of her father, a physics and mathematics teacher, Curie began her lifelong love affair with science.

By 1894, Curie had earned degrees in physics and mathematics from the Sorbonne in Paris. The following year she married Pierre Curie, another devoted scientist. Together they discovered two radioactive elements. (Radioactive elements are substances that release energy in the form of invisible rays).

Curie named the first element polonium, after her native Poland, and the second one radium. In 1903, the Curies shared the Nobel prize in physics for the discovery of radioactivity. In 1911, after her husband had died, Curie was awarded the Nobel Prize in chemistry for these discoveries, as well.

Curie made enormous advances in science throughout her life. She was especially pleased when radioactivity began to be used to treat cancer, a therapy that was called Curietherapy in her honor. Curie is considered the "Mother of the Atomic Age." She has remained an inspiration for generations, especially to women interested in science.

Marie Curie was the first woman to win a Nobel Prize in physics

FAREWELL, POLAND!

Polish peasants had strong ties to their homeland. In many cases, their families lived in the same area for generations. A village was often like one big extended family. Everyone knew everyone else, and the peasants were always willing to lend a hand if one of their neighbors met with disaster.

The peasants felt secure in their village; everything was familiar. They would say they were happy if after a day's work—even backbreaking work—they could return to a home where the children were healthy and there was enough food to eat.

But finding enough to eat became more and more difficult. By the late 1800s, the Polish population had skyrocketed. In many villages, the population had tripled in just 40 years! With so many people wanting land, how were the peasants ever going to afford their own farms? It was impossible. Parents divided their land among their sons. But if the parents had a

Polish peasants scratch for valuable salt near a burned warehouse

20-acre farm and five sons, that meant each son would only inherit a 4-acre farm. And what would the next generation do?

Letters from relatives in America persuaded many Poles to immigrate

Some of the best advertisements for the New Country were letters written by Poles in America to families back in Poland. A typical letter read: "In America, you sweat more in one day than you would in one week in Poland. But I wouldn't go back if someone was to give me the master's estate. Once you have tasted America, it is impossible to go back to those old miseries." Such letters persuaded many Poles to come to America, in search of a new and better life.

Some Polish women sold goods on city streets to earn money. This market is in Krakow.

One disaster followed another. Overcrowded villages became breeding grounds for diseases like cholera and typhus—which spread like wildfire throughout the country. To make matters worse, a strange fungus destroyed the potato plants in many parts of Poland, as it had in Ireland. Many people went hungry.

Many families were separated for months. Father often set out to find work in other parts of Poland. But wages were low and food prices were high. How was he going to feed his family?

Mother stayed at home. She took jobs washing and mending, and worried about her children. How could she afford to warm the house in the winter? Or pay for medicine if one of her children became ill? The older children helped with household chores and thought about their bleak future. How would they ever be able to marry, buy a farm, and raise a family?

Life was changing rapidly for the Polish peasants, and almost always for the worse. What were they going to do? There were rumors about a mythical place where the mountains were full of gold, where hard work was rewarded with a fair salary, where people could afford fine clothes and good food. It was a place far away called America.

At first, small numbers of single men braved the wide Atlantic Ocean to try their luck in the "New Country." Their scheme was to make quick money, then return to Poland to buy the large, prospering farms of their dreams.

But most Polish immigrants chose to stay in America, won over by the freedom and opportunity they found there. They urged family members still in Poland to join them, which began a process called "chain migration." By the 1880s, thousands of Poles escaped the poverty of their native land and made their way *do Ameryki*—"to America."

THE JAMESTOWN POLES

Although the majority of Polish immigrants came to the United States in the late 1800s, Poles had been coming to America since colonial times. In fact, Poles were among the nation's first immigrant settlers. They are known especially for the important contributions they made to the Jamestown colony.

Jamestown was originally founded in 1607 by 104 English colonists. But of these 104 colonists, only 12 were skilled workers. The rest were of the upper class, known as "gentlemen" in those days. They had never done any manual labor.

This was a great disadvantage, because life in the new colony was very hard. The colonists had to build homes, dig wells for fresh water, plant corn and vegetables, negotiate with Indian tribes, and hunt for food. But with only 12 workers, how were the colonists going to accomplish all of these tasks? In addition, they were expected to produce goods for shipment to England, which ruled the colony.

The colonists' problem was solved by Captain Christopher Newport. He knew that Poland had many capable artisans and regularly traded Polish-made goods with England. So, on October 1, 1608, when Captain Newport returned to Jamestown with supplies for the colonists, he also brought several Polish artisans.

The Polish artisans were an immense help to the new colony. As soon as they arrived, the Poles began digging wells, build-

Polish glass blowers began the first glass factory in the colonies

The Jamestown Poles were known for many "firsts." They built the first factory in America, produced the first goods for export to England, and staged the first strike for democratic rights. But while the Jamestown Poles were successfully fighting for human rights in 1619, the first shipload of African slaves landed in Virginia. There was no longer a demand for skilled artisans. Instead, the colonists began to plant tobacco, cotton, and other crops and to harvest these crops with the forced, unpaid labor of slaves.

*Workers labor to make Jamestown
a prospering colony*

ing better shelters, and clearing land. Soon, more Polish artisans were invited to the colony. The Jamestown Poles set up workshops in order to make pitch, tar, resin, soap, and other products for export to England. And just a few months later, the first factory in America was producing glass, a feat accomplished entirely by Polish workers.

But in 1619, the English colonists took an action that riled up the hardworking Poles. Governor Sir George Yeardley called for a meeting in the Jamestown church on July 30, 1619, to organize the first representative legislative body in America. This was an opportunity for the colonists to vote for the candidates who would best represent them in the new Jamestown government. Only native-born Englishmen were allowed to vote; the Poles were denied this basic right.

The Poles, who had contributed greatly to the growth of the colony, were furious. They demanded Governor Yeardley grant them the same democratic rights enjoyed by the English colonists. When their plea was refused, the Poles banded together and went on strike. No vote, no work, the Polish settlers said, and they shut down all of their glass, tar, and soap factories.

Their protest was effective because the work done by the Poles was so important to the colony. On July 21, 1619, just before the scheduled meeting, Governor Yeardley declared that the Jamestown Poles were entitled to the same freedoms as the English.

The Jamestown Poles won the right to vote! As a result, the Poles became the first ethnic group in America to organize a successful strike for civil rights.

*Jamestown colonists. Poles were among the first
non-English immigrants invited to the new colony.*

THE REVOLUTIONARY WAR

When the colonies declared their independence from Britain in 1776, many Poles raced to this country to help the colonies fight for freedom. The most noteworthy of these Poles were Thaddeus Kosciuszko (KOS-eh-US-koh) and Casimir Pułaski (puh-WAHS-kee).

Brigadier General Thaddeus Kosciuszko was born in Polish Lithuania on February 12, 1746. He was a top student in some of the best military academies in Europe. As a result, when Kosciuszko volunteered for the American army in 1776, he was one of George Washington's best-trained military engineers.

Kosciuszko built sea forts on Billingsport Island in order to prevent the British from entering the Delaware River.

He masterminded a brilliant defensive battle position at Bemis Heights, which forced the surrender of 6,300 British troops. He also fortified West Point so well that it was considered absolutely safe from British capture.

Kosciuszko spent his lifetime fighting for freedom both in Poland and in America. In 1828, a monument was raised at West Point, a military academy, in his honor with the inscription, "To the hero of two worlds."

Seven American counties, five towns, a highway, and many streets and schools are named for Brigadier General Casimir Pułaski, the "Father of the American Cavalry."

Pułaski was born into the nobility in 1747 in Winiary, a town 40 miles from Warsaw. He was a fierce Polish patriot and

Kosciuszko gave money for freeing and educating African American slaves

Kosciuszko did not have many possessions; he loved liberty above all. He admired the ancient Greek Timoleon because "he was able to restore his country's freedom, taking nothing for himself." Before he died in Switzerland on October 15, 1817, Kosciuszko willed that the money made from his American estates be used to free and educate African American slaves. Kosciuszko's actions caused his friend Thomas Jefferson to call him "the truest son of liberty I have ever known."

Pułaski led many battles against the British during the Revolutionary War

led many attacks against the invading Russians. However, when Poland was finally conquered, Pułaski was forced to leave his country in exile. Reminded of the lost independence of his homeland, Pułaski sympathized with the colonists' struggle for liberty. He met Benjamin Franklin in Paris in 1776, and volunteered to fight for colonial independence.

Pułaski planned many shrewd and successful attacks on the British army. In the Battle of Brandywine, Pułaski and thirty of his men charged the front lines of the British army. This maneuver allowed American soldiers to escape a British trap.

Pułaski also fought courageously in Germantown and Charleston, and he trained a group of cavalry called "The Pułaski Legion." During battle in Savannah, the Americans were losing to the British because their military plans had been revealed to the enemy by a traitor. Pułaski led his troops to safety, but not before he was shot in the thigh. He died that evening, on October 11, 1779.

Pułaski's bravery on the battlefield and his untimely death made him a much-loved hero of the American Revolution. He was idealistic, bold, and brave. Pułaski explained to George Washington that Poles like himself were willing to risk their lives for American independence because "wherever men can fight for liberty, that is also our fight and our place."

THE WAVE OF IMMIGRATION

For centuries, Poles had been coming to America in small numbers, but after 1880 they began to arrive in swarms. In fact, between 1880 and 1925 about 3 million Polish peasants immigrated to America!

The journey to America was often overwhelming to Polish peasants—most had never even traveled beyond their local villages! So you can imagine how scary it must have been for them to travel more than 4,000 miles to an unfamiliar country.

The peasants' journey to America took many steps. First, they traveled from their remote village to the nearest city, either on foot or by a horse-drawn cart. Next, they took a train to one of the major ports in Germany or Holland to meet their ship. Finally, full of dreams and hope, the peasants boarded their ships bound for America.

But the peasants still had a rough journey ahead of them. Most could afford only the cheapest fares. They were stuffed into dingy compartments below deck, called steerage. There, for the entire journey (usually 15 to 20 days) they lived in crowded and unsanitary conditions. Rough weather made everything even worse. Many immigrants got terribly seasick and had to stay in their beds.

When the sailing was smooth, however, the immigrants were so excited they complained little. They often made good friends on the trip and spent as much time as possible on deck, breathing in the fresh sea air. Adventuresome children explored the nooks and crannies of the ship, and often snitched some of the fine food served to the passengers in first class.

UPI/Bettmann Newsphotos

At Ellis Island, immigrants were sometimes offered food they had never tasted before

Can you imagine going on the long journey from Poland to America all by yourself? Many Polish girls and boys—some as young as 12 years old—traveled to America alone to join relatives already there. Usually, adults accompanied them only to the nearest train station. After that, the young people traveled the rest of the way alone. They wore a sign on their chest bearing their name and where they were going in many different languages.

By the mid-1880s, the Statue of Liberty had been built. It greeted the millions of immigrants who sailed into New York Harbor. When the weary immigrants first glimpsed this famous symbol of freedom, they began to cry, dance, rejoice, and pray. They had finally made it to America!

After 1892, the immigrant ships landed at Ellis Island in New York Harbor. Here, the newcomers had to pass a number of "tests" before they could start their life in America. First, they were given a medical exam to make sure they did not have any diseases, such as tuberculosis or trachoma, an eye disease that eventually causes blindness. If they did, they were immediately sent back to Poland.

Then they met with an

The Statue of Liberty was a symbol of freedom for many immigrants

immigration official who asked questions like, "Who are you?" "Where are you going?" "What skills do you have?" "How much money do you have?"

This questioning bewildered and frightened the new immigrants, most of whom did not speak English. What was happening? The immigrants thought they had landed in paradise, only to be shoved into a huge, crowded building, pushed from one line to another, and bombarded with questions!

But the majority of immigrants did not have any serious problems at Ellis Island. By the following day, they were free to join their relatives—or make their own way in their new land. For them, one journey had finally ended, and a new one had just begun.

The immigrants had to pass a medical exam before they could enter the New Country

25

WORK IN THE NEW COUNTRY

After leaving Ellis Island, most immigrants had only enough money to last a couple of weeks—then they would be out on the streets. But proud Polish immigrants did not come to the "land of opportunity" to wind up as beggars. So their next challenge was to find work.

In fact, millions of immigrants were able to come to America because unskilled jobs were easy to find. By the late 1800s,

Pennsylvania coal mines employed thousands of Polish immigrants

Culver Pictures

America was a booming industrial country, and factories popped up in the northeastern cities at lightning speed. Many jobs that took skill and experience had been replaced with machines. What America needed now was muscle-power, and plenty of it. The endless flow of immigrants supplied this power.

Most Polish immigrants came to America straight from their village farms without special skills, savings, or formal education. However, they did have muscle-power—and a hearty willingness to work. But all they could find in America were backbreaking jobs in sweltering factories that made their lives back in Poland seem easy.

Polish men worked 10- to 12-hour days in the noisy automobile shops of Detroit, the cold slaughterhouses of Chicago, and the sooty coal mines of Pennsylvania. They swung their picks and heaved their shovels throughout the streets and sewers of the

Not all Polish immigrants gave up the plow and spade of the Old World for the pick and shovel of the New; about 20 percent remained farmers. These Poles turned thousands of New England farms, thought too poor to grow anything, into thriving onion and tobacco fields—which brought in a good deal of money! In fact, President Calvin Coolidge admitted that it took the Polish immigrants to show the Yankees how to till the soil.

cities. They toiled away in foundries so hot, their clothes sometimes caught on fire. These new immigrants worked the longest hours in the dirtiest jobs—for which they were paid only $1 or $2 a day.

Polish women were taught to care for the home. But in America, many labored in suffocating garment factories. They worked 10-hour days sewing shirts, making hats, or finishing blouses—for only 60¢ to $1.10 per dozen. Others worked in the slicing rooms of tin-can factories, where they often had their fingers cut off by the unsafe machinery.

Unmarried Polish girls worked "maiding" (as maids) for wealthy families. This was one of the least popular jobs. The young girls were cooped up in a strange house and were expected to work 12 hours a day, six or seven days a week. They had no time to explore America, meet with friends, or learn the language. One Polish maid lived in America for eight weeks before she had a chance to visit her uncle—who lived only three blocks away!

The Polish immigrants suffered greatly, and many became ill from their heavy workload. But by and large the Poles were optimistic—they refused to give up on

Many Polish American women worked long hours in clothing factories

their American dream. They took night classes to learn English, and tried to find better jobs with higher wages.

Families saved every penny possible. They used these savings first to bring over relatives still in Poland, and then to buy their own store, bakery, business, house, or land. It often cost a lifetime of work, but the Polish immigrants were determined to find their fortune in America.

Meat packing plants in Chicago provided many Polish immigrants with jobs

PREJUDICE

olish immigrants quickly found themselves in a no-win situation. They couldn't speak English, had no special training, and were running out of money. Labor contractors took advantage of the immigrants' poverty and only offered them jobs if they worked for less money. The Poles took these jobs out of desperation—and then were hated by many Americans who believed these Polish immigrants were stealing *their* jobs.

As a result, Polish immigrants met prejudice wherever they went. Fathers were beaten up by angry co-workers, harassed by supervisors, or denied their wages. Mothers were ridiculed at stores and markets when they struggled to make their purchases in broken English. Children often came home from school in tears. Their classmates teased them because of their accent, the way they dressed, or just because they were "different." Many Polish children became ashamed of their Polish roots.

Newspapers were full of hurtful stories about the immigrants. These stories complained of the "mixed populations," meaning people from other countries. Grocers and butchers made a habit of charging Polish customers up to five times more than English or Irish customers.

Even worse, employers stereotyped Polish immigrants, especially women, as strong, tough, and capable of the most backbreaking work. As a result, Poles were given the heaviest and dirtiest jobs. One employer said he preferred hiring Polish

Officials at Ellis Island sometimes changed Polish immigrants' last names

Unfortunately, prejudice against Polish Americans still exists today. Racist "Polish jokes" are commonly told. These jokes are hurtful to Polish Americans, especially children. In addition, many successful Polish Americans have felt it necessary to change their last names to ones that do not sound Polish. Other ethnic groups have done this, too. In fact, immigration officials at Ellis Island often changed the last names of Polish and other European immigrants. They did this because they could not pronounce the immigrants' names and wanted to "Americanize" the immigrants. Would you want someone to change your last name? More and more Polish Americans are now proudly taking back their true last names.

Polish immigrant women were often given very hard jobs. This old woman is stripping tobacco.

women because "they are hard workers and don't object to scrubbing tiled floors on their knees." Another said that Polish women were "equal to heavy jobs," as if they were mules, not human beings.

Some of the worst cases of prejudice occurred in the coal-mining regions of Pennsylvania. There, between 1880 and 1900, the Polish population increased from just 2,000 to 38,000. Most of these new Polish immigrants were recruited to work in the dangerous, sooty coal mines. They were promised fair wages they never received. And in the end, they lived in rickety shanties more run-down than the cattle shelters back in Poland.

To make matters worse, in 1888 the miners of the Shenandoah Valley, most of whom were Polish, had their meager wages cut without reason. This time the miners fought back—they went on strike. But the strike was crushed with violence. On February 3, deputies fired into a crowd of 500 peaceful picketers. Twelve miners were shot down. The newspapers, which thought the Polish strikers were being ungrateful, praised the deputies.

Violence was used again during the Lattimer Massacre of 1897. On September 6 of that year, a large group of miners marched to protest the unfair labor practices of the mining companies. Although the protesters were not armed, 100 deputies fired into the crowd to, as they said, "disarm a rebellious mob." Fifty-eight strikers were either killed or wounded, 26 of whom were Poles. There was an investigation, but all of the officials involved were found innocent.

Polish American coal miners in Pennsylvania faced the most violent acts of prejudice

COMMUNITY LIFE

Homesickness, language barriers, and prejudice made the Polish immigrants cling to each other. They realized that if they lived side by side with other Poles, at least they would not have to face discrimination in their own neighborhoods. As a result, "Little Polands" sprang up in all the cities where large groups of Polish immigrants settled.

However, Polish neighborhoods were far from paradise. The new immigrants made very little money and so were forced to move into run-down shanty towns where they could find inexpensive housing. In the cities, entire families of 8, 10, or 12 people often lived in one room, sometimes without even one window to let in fresh air and sunlight.

In the mining towns, the living conditions were even worse. Here, the immigrants built their houses with their own

Chicago Historical Society

Polish American children, such as these kids in Chicago, played freely in their neighborhoods

The neighborhood pisennik *wrote letters for community members who could not read or write*

An interesting member of the Polish neighborhood was the *pisennik* (pi-SEHN-ick)—the local scribe who knew how to read and write. Most of the first Polish immigrants who came to America were illiterate. So when they wanted to send a letter back home, they would go to the local *pisennik* and tell him or her what to write. Imagine how embarrassing it was for the young man or woman who wanted to send a love letter to a sweetheart back in Poland! They had to declare their love to the *pisennik* before it could be sent to their loved ones.

Literary circles, like this one in Chicago, were formed to discuss Polish literature and language

hands. They could not afford proper building material, so they built their walls from discarded boards and rubble found along the highway. They made their roofs with tin pressed from empty cans. These huts were freezing in the winter, and few families could afford enough fuel to keep a fire going through the long winter nights.

But like it or not, these were the only places the Polish immigrants could call home, and they were going to make the best of it. In the cities, mothers turned their dirty hovels into clean and healthy homes. Empty lots and unused alleys were made into makeshift gardens, and each year many families had a small harvest of fresh, home-grown vegetables.

In the mining towns, neglected backyards were turned into thriving farms. Families kept pigs and chickens whenever possible and grew potatoes, cabbages, and onions as they had in the old days back in Poland. The children helped with chores, or romped through the countryside in search of wild huckleberries.

In their own neighborhoods, Polish immigrants were treated with dignity and respect. Mother could make her purchases from Polish butchers, bakers, and grocers who were sure to stock plenty of Polish food. She no longer had to worry about being mocked or cheated. Father could relax in the local tavern, surrounded by the familiar sounds of his own language. He could find support with other Poles experiencing the same hardships. Children could attend schools run by Polish nuns, where they would not be teased for wearing tattered clothes or speaking broken English.

The immigrants felt a sense of belonging in Polish neighborhoods. Aunts, cousins, brothers and sisters, and parents often lived within a few blocks of each other. Children were free to run through the streets—but if they were caught up to no good, they could be sure their mothers would find out. Everyone knew everyone else. And if a family met with misfortune, all the neighbors would pitch in and help out in any way they could.

THE CATHOLIC CHURCH

he vast majority of Polish immigrants were Catholic. Priests and parishioners came to America side by side, and together they strove to build a thriving religious life in the New Country.

But in America, Mass was said in English (which many immigrants did not understand), and Polish religious customs were completely ignored. The Polish immigrants wanted to worship in a church where the priests respected their religious customs and cared about their special problems.

So the Poles began a crusade to build their own churches. The immigrants were very poor, but they skimped and saved and willingly turned over every last penny to their priests. Within a few years, huge, beautiful churches sprang up in almost every

Polish shanty town, like giant sunflowers growing from a pile of rubble. These churches were symbols of pride for the Poles because they were built with their own effort and money.

The Poles eventually built more than 900 churches, each one with its own school, convent, and social programs. The church soon became the proud center of community life. Polish children were taught in its schools, families danced and played within its roomy halls, and the entire community prayed under its high, awe-inspiring ceilings.

However, the success of Polish Catholic life created tensions and difficulties between the Poles and other American

---

In the fall of 1978 Poland's Karol Wojtyla (voy-TEH-wah) became Pope John Paul II. Polish Americans, who felt a special kinship with the new pope, wept and cheered with pride. Called the "Philosopher Pope," the "Poet Pope," and the "People's Pope," John Paul II is greatly loved. He is the first pope to travel widely and has met with leaders throughout the world. He urges people to practice kindness and asks nations to follow strict ethical standards, which are rules to tell right from wrong. His message for the world is for peace. When he is greeted by crowds chanting, "John Paul II, we love you," the pope gently replies, "John Paul II, he loves you."

Reuters/Bettmann

John Paul II, *the first Polish Pope, greets* Lech Wałęsa, *president of Poland*

Polish parishioners prepare to build their first community church in Binghamton, New York, 1914

Catholics. Many of the leaders in the American Catholic Church (who were mostly Irish or German) believed the use of the Polish language for church services and school instruction was "un-Catholic" and "un-American." They said that ethnic differences among Catholics should be ironed out by "Americanizing" the Church and abandoning all European customs.

Because of this, the contributions of many Polish priests were never recognized by the American Catholic Church as a whole. For example, in 1886 there were 69 bishops in the American Church. Thirty-five were Irish, 15 were German, and 11 were French. Not one bishop was of Polish descent, even though Poles made up almost 20 percent of the entire American Catholic population!

The Poles were angry that they were being excluded from the Church's upper ranks. So in 1897, Father Francis Hodur broke with the American Catholic Church and established the Polish National Church of America. Finally, priests and parishioners had a say in how their parishes were run. By 1904, over 20,000 Polish Catholics became members of this new denomination, and Father Hodur was elected its first bishop.

The success of the Polish National Church forced the Pope in Rome to realize that Polish Catholics deserved to be recognized and represented in the American Catholic Church. Over the next 60 years, nine priests of Polish descent rose to the rank of bishop, and Archbishop John Krol of Philadelphia became the first Polish American cardinal; Edmund Szoka became the second. Archbishop Adam Maida, the current head of the Archdiocese of Detroit, speaks fluent Polish.

Easter Mass in Buffalo, New York, 1943

FAMOUS POLISH AMERICANS

Marie Zakrzewska (1829–1890)

During the 1800s, women were prevented from becoming physicians and medical researchers. Marie Zakrzewska (zhahk-JEHF-skah), like her mother before her, wanted to become a doctor. But European women could only become midwives, meaning they were limited to delivering babies. So at 18, Marie attended the college of midwifery in Berlin, in what is now Germany.

Then Marie heard that in America women could become full doctors of medicine. Full of hopes and dreams, she immigrated to America. Three years later, she received her medical degree, only to find the door of opportunity slammed in her face. In America women could become doctors, but they could not work in hospitals!

Marie was furious. She was determined to fight discrimination against women in medicine. She tirelessly asked wealthy society women for donations and support, and in 1859 she triumphantly opened the New England Hospital for Women and Children in Boston. The hospital was run by women and for women, and included the first American professional school for nurses.

Marie also demanded professional training for African American women. She urged black women to enter the medical field, a controversial action that almost ended her career. The first black nurse in America, Mary Elizabeth Mahoney, graduated from Marie's school in 1879. And Dr. Caroline V. Still, one of the first black women doctors, got her start in the Boston hospital.

Stan Musial (b. 1920)

Ever wonder what it would be like to be a famous baseball player? This was Stan Musial's dream—one that came true. Stan was a "natural" from the moment he began playing baseball in high school, and he wanted to become a professional. But his parents wanted him to go to college. Finally, Stan convinced his parents to give him a chance at the major league. He knocked their socks off with his success.

Stan Musial became one of the most famous baseball players in history, and cer-

Marie Zakrzewska founded the New England Hospital for Women and Children in Boston

Stan Musial was elected to the Baseball Hall of Fame in 1969

tainly the most famous player of Polish descent. From 1941 to 1963, Stan played outfield and first base for the St. Louis Cardinals, and his career was studded with highlights. He was voted the most valuable player of the National League three times, in 1943, 1946, and 1948, and he won seven National League batting titles. In honor of such a spectacular career, in 1969 Stan Musial was elected to the Baseball Hall of Fame in Cooperstown, New York.

Zbigniew Brzezinski (b. 1928)

Zbigniew Brzezinski (SBIG-nee-ev bje-ZIN-ski) was born in Warsaw, but moved to America with his family as a boy. His father was a Polish diplomat, and Brzezinski grew up surrounded by the buzz of political discussions. He became interested in politics himself, and went on to earn a Ph.D in govern-ment from Harvard University. He has been a key player in American politics for decades.

Brzezinski is considered one of the best American experts on the communist government of the former Soviet Union. During the years of the Cold War, when relations between the United States and the former Soviet Union were tense, Brzezinski's advice and expertise was sought by three different presidents. He has filled many top government positions. He is now a professor of foreign affairs at Johns Hopkins University in Baltimore, Maryland.

In addition, Brzezinski has published many books and articles dealing with communism and American foreign policy and has won the respect of leaders throughout the world. He has proved that "America is a place where a man called Zbigniew Brzezinski can make a name for himself without even changing it."

Zbigniew Brzezinski is an expert on U.S. relations with the former Soviet Union

WORLD WAR II

On September 1, 1939, Germany invaded Poland using what were called *blitzkrieg*, or "lightning war," tactics. The invasion began World War II. All major Polish cities were bombed again and again. The Poles fought back valiantly, but they lacked the weapons needed to combat Germany's Nazi war machine. By the end of the war, the German army had killed 7 million Poles, a fifth of Poland's population. Among these were nearly all of Poland's 3 million Jews. The Nazis killed Poles in concentration camps and through mass executions, massacres, and starvation.

In the United States, news of Germany's brutal invasion of Poland sent shock waves through Polish American communities. Well over 100,000 American Poles marched up New York's Fifth Avenue during the Pułaski Day Parade. Both the marchers and the spectators, whether Polish or not, wept at the violence being done to innocent Polish citizens. Polish Americans wanted to fight for their native homeland.

The Bettmann Archive

Many Polish American women worked in munitions factories

In fact, thousands of Polish Americans fought for Poland even before the United States entered the war. One of these was 17-year-old Lieutenant Bronislaw Godlewski of

After World War II, more than 150,000 Poles fled Poland for America

After World War II the Polish government was quickly taken over by the communist former Soviet Union. Many members of the Polish resistance—who believed in democracy—were unable to return to their homeland. As a result, over 150,000 Polish war victims and refugees immigrated to America. But since immigration laws had become very strict, this was the last large wave of Poles allowed to enter the United States.

Many relief programs were organized by Polish Americans. Here, bundles of clothing are collected for war-torn Poland.

Chicago. He began fighting immediately with the Polish Air Force. He eventually earned medals from Poland, Britain, and America for his courage in battle.

But once America did enter World War II, after the Japanese attacked Pearl Harbor in 1941, more than 1 million Polish Americans eagerly joined the United States Armed Forces. They fought bravely out of loyalty to both their former homeland and the United States.

For example, William Grabiarz volunteered for the Army at age 18 and participated in five great battles in the Pacific. For his bravery he was awarded nine awards, among them the Congressional Medal of Honor—the nation's highest. Colonel Francis S. Gabreski became America's ace of aces by shooting down 31 German planes. He won 12 Distinguished Flying Crosses and went on to participate in the Korean War.

But many other Polish American heroes of World War II showed courage and patriotism while remaining in their hometowns. These were the women of the war. Polish American women prepared bandages, vol-unteered for the Red Cross, and organized relief efforts for Polish war victims. They left their homes and worked long hours in war factory assembly lines. They formed knitting circles that made blankets and warm clothing for the servicemen overseas. And as nurses and medical professionals, they assisted wounded soldiers.

In addition, American Poles contributed generously to the War effort. For example, during the Fourth and Fifth War Loan Drive in Chicago, Polish Americans bought $34 million in war bonds, more than any other ethnic group. Buying war bonds was important because the government used this money to purchase bombers, tanks, and ammunition. In Pennsylvania, Mrs. Francis P. Tarnapowicz alone sold $270 million in bonds to 101 Polish groups.

World War II created a strong sense of national unity in the United States. Polish Americans proved to be generous, brave, and patriotic soldiers and citizens. They returned from battle not as foreigners, but as national heroes who risked their lives for the common good of all Americans.

CHICAGO, "AMERICA'S WARSAW"

Ever since the 1860s, Polish immigrants began establishing little Polish "colonies" in Chicago. The immigrants were lured to the city by the demand for unskilled labor. They found jobs in the garment-making shops of the northwest side, the slaughterhouses on the west side, and the steel plants on the south side.

At first, the life of the Chicago Poles differed little from other Polish immigrants. But soon the Poles not only lived in their Chicago neighborhoods, they began to own them as well. By the early 1900s Polish immigrants purchased about 70 percent of all property put up for sale in Chicago.

The Poles were able to buy their own property by forming Polish building and loan societies. The societies were like small local banks. They usually grew out of meetings held in a church or saloon, where group members shared information on buying a home.

Members made small weekly contributions to these societies, about 25¢ a week in 1886 to about $2.50 a week by 1910. After five or so years, the members could withdraw their money, with interest, and use it for a down payment for a house.

The success of the Polish immigrants in Chicago drew many other Poles to the area. In fact, by 1920 more than 400,000 Polish Americans lived in Chicago—more than any other place except Poland itself. Besides, Chicago was a city where Polish immigrants could settle without suffering "culture shock"—confusion caused by unfamiliar American customs and language.

Chicago Historical Society

Headquarters for a Polish American organization in 1890

Today, Chicago still boasts a 40-block Polish American business district, a huge number of Polish American organizations, and a Polka Music Hall of Fame. The business district continues to serve both new immigrants and many second-, third-, and fourth-generation Polish Americans who have remained in the Chicago area.

Polish Americans owned many of the stores and homes in their neighborhoods

In "America's Warsaw"—a nickname for Chicago—Poles were surrounded by what was familiar. Polish bakers sold delicious black bread and rye bread, baked just like it was in the Old Country. They made tasty Polish treats like gingerbread, jam cookies, baba, or *chruściki* (hrush-CHEE-kee)—a delicious fried, airy dough topped with powdered sugar.

Butchers sold *kielbasa* (keel-BAH-sah), the now-famous Polish sausage. Grocers stocked many Polish newspapers, journals, and periodicals. And the smell of favorite Polish dishes, like *bigos* (BEE-gohs) and *pierogis* (peer-oh-GEES), filled the neighborhood streets with the familiar scent of home.

Poles also loved the pomp and splendor of parades. So, on October 7, 1893, the first annual Polish Day parade marched throughout the streets of Chicago. The parade was led by 16 uniformed Polish policemen, followed by respected community leaders, children in colorful Polish costume, and men of the military societies in blue, red, and gold uniforms. Trailing the procession were 16 floats gloriously decorated with flowers. More than 50,000 Polish Americans participated in the parade, twice as many watched, and the Chicago Poles beamed with community pride.

Polish American life in Chicago was also enriched by the many Polish groups that aided new immigrants. Some of these organizations offered education, such as English language or citizenship classes. Others, however, wanted to preserve and celebrate Polish culture, or just have a good time. And for Polish Americans, that often meant a good polka party.

Although the polka was originally a Czech dance, Polish Americans soon adopted it as their own. One of the most famous polka masters was Chicago's own Li'l Wally, a one-man-band. He beat drums with his feet, played the accordion, and merrily sang while thousands of Polish Americans danced till dawn.

Even today Chicago still boasts a thriving Polish American community

FINDING THE AMERICAN DREAM

Throughout all of their hardships, the Polish immigrants never lost hope. They were constantly driven by the American Dream. To the Poles, this simply meant earning a decent living and knowing their children had the world ahead of them and would not be denied any opportunities.

It took many generations of hard work before even this simple dream became a reality. But gradually Polish Americans got ahead. The first generation of Polish Americans saved only about $50 a year, but over the years their small savings grew into a tidy sum.

Most Polish Americans bought their own homes. This was a day filled with tears and pride, because the immigrants finally had something to show for their years of backbreaking work. Other families decided to put their savings into a family business. They became bakers, butchers, grocers, shoemakers, or store owners.

The Kosciuszko Foundation

Beginning with a one-truck business in 1918, Joseph Slotkowski's sausage company is now the largest in the Chicago area

Senator Barbara Ann Mikulski was one of the first women elected to Congress

Senator Barbara Ann Mikulski once said, "My great-grandmother came to America from Poland at age 16 with no money or job, looking for opportunity." Mikulski inherited her great-grandmother's courage and entered politics because she knew she could make a difference. She became the first Democratic woman to serve in both houses of Congress and to win a statewide election in Maryland. She was also one of the first women to win a seat in the United States Senate. Through her intelligence, humor, and kindness, Senator Mikulski has made great strides in politics for both women and Polish Americans.

40

Five Polish American women joyfully prepare for a community member's wedding, 1947

Second-generation Poles usually finished high school. They had more opportunities than their parents, but also more confusions. Who were they? They felt Polish in their neighborhoods, but American in their schools. Were they Polish, American, or both?

Many second-generation Polish Americans ended their confusion by living near their families and neighborhoods, but finding work that paid well. They entered the police force, volunteered as fire fighters, or held city jobs. Or—like Edmund Muskie—they made politics their career.

Edmund Muskie was the son of a Polish immigrant tailor. In 1954, Muskie became the governor of Maine, and after two terms he went on to become a United States Senator.

In 1968, presidential candidate Hubert Humphrey chose Senator Muskie as his running-mate during the Democratic Convention. When the Humphrey-Muskie ticket was defeated by Richard Nixon in the November election, Muskie returned to the Senate.

By the third generation, around the 1950s, more and more Polish Americans were going to college. Polish Americans had entered almost all professions. They found jobs in banking, education, medicine, film, publishing, and engineering.

One successful Polish American is Stephen Wozniak, the co-founder of Apple Computer, Inc. His multi-million dollar company began in a garage! Wozniak now spends much of his time teaching kids in California how to use computers and how they work.

As Polish American communities grew stronger, Polish American women became increasingly outspoken. They also wanted a chance to pursue the opportunities America offered. They demanded an education equal to men's and the right to a career. Soon, Polish American women became a respected part of the work force.

By the late 1950s, the walls that separated Polish Americans from mainstream American life had come crumbling down. The battle had lasted for generations, but Polish Americans finally won the freedoms and opportunities promised to all American citizens.

THE POLISH AMERICAN

Since the Jamestown Poles came to America in the 1600s, about 3 million Poles have immigrated to the United States. Today, the largest numbers of Polish Americans live in such cities as Chicago, New York, Detroit, Philadelphia, and Buffalo.

Surprisingly, however, many Polish immigrants only began to feel "Polish" once they *came* to America. Back in the Old Country, most Polish peasants felt loyal mainly to their town or village. They thought of themselves as from the Silesian region in the west or from the mountain region in the south, rather than from Poland itself.

But in the New Country, the hustle and bustle of cities and the sound of the English language were foreign to the Polish immigrants. The newcomers yearned for the familiar. They felt most at home with other Poles—no matter what region they were from!

From their very beginnings in this country, Polish American communities have struggled to keep Polish customs and traditions alive. Even today, there are a large number of organizations that work to preserve Polish heritage. Thousands of Polish cultural, religious, and historical societies are scattered throughout the country.

Even though Poland won independence after World War II, it was taken over by the communist government of the former Soviet Union. As a result, most Polish citizens were denied basic freedoms and democratic rights. But in the 1980s, an independent trade union called Solidarity was formed. It was led by a man named Lech Wałęsa (lehk vah-WEHN-sah). The Solidarity movement organized Polish laborers against the communist government and was eventually successful. But at first, the laborers' strikes and protests were brutally crushed. Some Poles fled to America, but many others continued struggling for freedom in Poland.

During this time of crisis, many Polish Americans became very concerned about the fate of Poland. They organized relief efforts to help Polish workers, sending more than $100 million in aid to Poland. The communist government was overthrown, and in 1990, Wałęsa was elected president of Poland.

Reuters/Bettmann

Lech Wałęsa supporters with a Solidarity banner, 1990

Many of these organizations have a large membership and are still going strong. The Polish American Historical Society is devoted to research on the history of Polish Americans. The Paderewski Foundation helps start departments for Polish studies in colleges and universities. And the Kosciuszko Foundation gives scholarships and sponsors exchange students between the United States and Poland.

Polish Americans have also created their own educational community at the Orchard Lake Schools in Orchard Lake, Michigan. Orchard Lake began as a seminary to educate Polish priests, who were needed to serve the growing number of Polish American parishes throughout the country. Today the seminary works side by side with St. Mary's College, a Catholic liberal arts college, and St. Mary's Preparatory School for boys. Together, they offer programs that promote Polish culture and pride. For example, they celebrate different aspects of Polish heritage on "Polish Day" each month, broadcast Mass over the radio in Polish, and have a library with a collection of 8,000 Polish books. They also sponsor workshops on Polish language, customs, history, and folk culture.

Many Polish Americans continued to care deeply about their native Poland, even after they were established in America. When Germany invaded Poland and began World War II, a greater percentage of Polish Americans volunteered for the Army than any other ethnic group. Most of these volunteers were second- or third-generation Polish Americans who had never even set foot in Poland! But they felt a special kinship with their ancestral homeland, as many Americans of Polish descent still do today.

First- and second-generation Polish Americans spent their lives in factories and sweatshops because they believed that their hard work would earn them, or at least their children, a better life. Their hard work has paid off.

Polish Americans have blended smoothly into American life. They have found work as teachers, doctors, scientists,

Polish Americans have gone far in many professions

A folk dance group performs at a Polish American festival

and businesspeople. Their children eat pizza, play baseball, and take piano lessons just like other kids. Like many Americans, Polish American children may have other ethnic roots as well. Perhaps you know someone who is—or you are yourself—half-Polish, one-quarter Irish, one-eighth English, with a sprinkling of German and Russian!

Today, the early struggles of Polish immigrants are passed on in stories told generation after generation. Polish Americans can now look back with pride on a long journey that has finally come to an end.

Polish American kids often learn about their heritage from their grandparents

INDEX

Other books about Polish Americans:

Kuniczak, W. S. *My Name is Million*. New York: Doubleday & Co., 1978.

Nowakowski, Jacek, ed. *Polish American Ways*. New York: Harper & Row, 1989.

Toor, Rachel. *The Polish Americans*. New York: Chelsea House, 1988.

Wytrwal, Joseph Anthony. *The Poles in America*. Minneapolis: Lerner Publications, 1969.

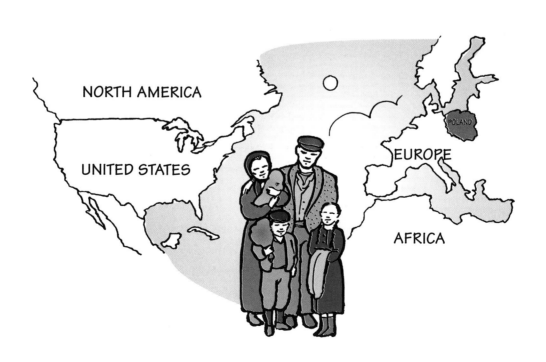

EXTREMELY WEIRD SERIES

*A*ll of the titles are written by Sarah Lovett, 8½" x 11", 48 pages, $9.95 paperbacks, with color photographs and illustrations

Extremely Weird Bats
Extremely Weird Birds
Extremely Weird Endangered Species
Extremely Weird Fishes
Extremely Weird Frogs
Extremely Weird Insects
Extremely Weird Mammals
Extremely Weird Micro Monsters
Extremely Weird Primates
Extremely Weird Reptiles
Extremely Weird Sea Creatures
Extremely Weird Snakes
Extremely Weird Spiders

X-RAY VISION SERIES

*E*ach title in the series is 8½" x 11", 48 pages, $9.95 paperback, with color photographs and illustrations, and written by Ron Schultz.

Looking Inside the Brain
Looking Inside Cartoon Animation
Looking Inside Caves and Caverns
Looking Inside Sports Aerodynamics
Looking Inside Sunken Treasure
Looking Inside Telescopes and the Night Sky

THE KIDDING AROUND TRAVEL GUIDES

*A*ll of the titles listed below are 64 pages and $9.95 paperbacks, except for *Kidding Around the National Parks* and *Kidding Around Spain*, which are 108 pages and $12.95 paperbacks.

Kidding Around Atlanta
Kidding Around Boston, 2nd ed.
Kidding Around Chicago, 2nd ed.
Kidding Around the Hawaiian Islands
Kidding Around London
Kidding Around Los Angeles
Kidding Around the National Parks
 of the Southwest
Kidding Around New York City, 2nd ed.
Kidding Around Paris
Kidding Around Philadelphia
Kidding Around San Diego
Kidding Around San Francisco
Kidding Around Santa Fe
Kidding Around Seattle
Kidding Around Spain
Kidding Around Washington, D.C., 2nd ed.

MASTERS OF MOTION SERIES

*E*ach title in the series is 10¼" x 9", 48 pages, $9.95 paperback, with color photographs and illustrations.

How to Drive an Indy Race Car
 David Rubel
How to Fly a 747
 Tim Paulson
How to Fly the Space Shuttle
 Russell Shorto

THE KIDS EXPLORE SERIES

*E*ach title is written by kids for kids by the Westridge Young Writers Workshop, 7" x 9", and $9.95 paperback, with photographs and illustrations by the kids.

Kids Explore America's Hispanic Heritage
112 pages
Kids Explore America's African American Heritage 128 pages
Kids Explore the Gifts of Children with Special Needs 128 pages
Kids Explore America's Japanese American Heritage 144 pages

ENVIRONMENTAL TITLES

Habitats: *Where the Wild Things Live*
Randi Hacker and Jackie Kaufman
8½" x 11", 48 pages, color illustrations, $9.95 paper

The Indian Way: *Learning to Communicate with Mother Earth*
Gary McLain
7" x 9", 114 pages, two-color illustrations, $9.95 paper

Rads, Ergs, and Cheeseburgers: *The Kids' Guide to Energy and the Environment*
Bill Yanda
7" x 9", 108 pages, two-color illustrations, $13.95 paper

The Kids' Environment Book: *What's Awry and Why*
Anne Pedersen
7" x 9",192 pages, two-color illustrations, $13.95 paper

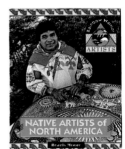

BIZARRE & BEAUTIFUL SERIES

A spirited and fun investigation of the mysteries of the five senses in the animal kingdom.

Each title in the series is 8½" x 11", $14.95 hardcover, with color photographs and illustrations throughout.

Bizarre & Beautiful Ears
Bizarre & Beautiful Eyes
Bizarre & Beautiful Feelers
Bizarre & Beautiful Noses
Bizarre & Beautiful Tongues

RAINBOW WARRIOR SERIES

W hat is a Rainbow Warrior Artist? It is a person who strives to live in harmony with the Earth and all living creatures, and who tries to better the world while living his or her life in a creative way.

Each title is written by Reavis Moore with a foreword by LeVar Burton, and is 8½" x 11", 48 pages, $14.95 hardcover, with color photographs and illustrations.

Native Artists of Africa
Native Artists of North America
Native Artists of Europe (available 9/94)

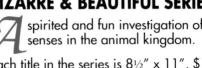

ROUGH AND READY SERIES

L earn about the men and women who settled the American West. Explore the myths and legends about these courageous individuals and learn about the environmental, cultural, and economic legacies they left to us.

Each title in the series is written by A. S. Gintzler and is 48 pages, 8½" x 11", $12.95 hardcover, with two-color illustrations and duotone archival photographs.

Available 7/94:

Rough and Ready Cowboys
Rough and Ready Homesteaders
Rough and Ready Prospectors

Rough and Ready Loggers
Rough and Ready
 Outlaws & Lawmen
Rough and Ready Railroaders

AMERICAN ORIGINS SERIES

M any of us are the third and fourth generation of our families to live in America. Learn what our great-great-grandparents experienced when they arrived here and how much of our lives are still intertwined with theirs.

Each title is 48 pages, 8½" x 11", $12.95 hardcover, with two-color illustrations and duotone archival photographs.

Available 6/94:

Tracing Our German Roots
Tracing Our Irish Roots
Tracing Our Italian Roots
Tracing Our Jewish Roots

Tracing Our Chinese Roots
Tracing Our Japanese Roots
Tracing Our Polish Roots

ORDERING INFORMATION
Please check your local bookstore for our books, or call 1-800-888-7504 to order direct from us. All orders are shipped via UPS; see chart below to calculate your shipping charge for U.S. destinations. **No P.O. Boxes please; we must have a street address to ensure delivery.** If the book you request is not available, we will hold your check until we can ship it. Foreign orders will be shipped surface rate unless otherwise requested; please enclose $3.00 for the first item and $1.00 for each additional item.

METHOD OF PAYMENT
Check, money order, American Express, MasterCard, or VISA. We cannot be responsible for cash sent through the mail. For credit card orders, include your card number, expiration date, and your signature, or call 1-800-888-7504. American Express card orders can be shipped only to billing address of card holder. Sorry, no C.O.D.'s. Residents of sunny New Mexico, add 6.25% tax to total.

Address all orders and inquiries to: John Muir Publications
P.O. Box 613
Santa Fe, NM 87504

(505) 982-4078
(800) 888-7504

For U.S. Orders Totaling	Add
Up to $15.00	$4.25
$15.01 to $45.00	$5.25
$45.01 to $75.00	$6.25
$75.01 or more	$7.25

DATE DUE